TATISA NEW-GENERATION AFRICAN POETS
A CHAPBOOK BOX SET

INTRODUCTION BY
KWAME DAWES & CHRIS ABANI

No part of this book may be reproduced, stored in a retrieval system, or transmitted in any form, by any means, including mechanical, electronic, photocopying, recording, or otherwise, without the prior written consent of the publisher.

Published by Akashic Books
©2023 Kwame Dawes and Chris Abani

ISBN for full box set: 978-1-63614-076-6
Library of Congress Control Number for full box set: 2022933682

All rights reserved
Printed in China
First printing

Akashic Books
Brooklyn, New York
Instagram, Twitter, Facebook: AkashicBooks
E-mail: info@akashicbooks.com
Website: www.akashicbooks.com

African Poetry Book Fund
Prairie Schooner
University of Nebraska
110 Andrews Hall
Lincoln, Nebraska 68588

*For Lorna,
Sena, Kekeli, and Akua,
Mama the Great,
and the tribe: Gwyneth, Kojo, Adjoa, Kojovi.
Remembering Aba and Neville.
K.D.*

*

*Remembering Daphne, Michael, and Greg,
and for Mark, Charles, Stella—my family.
I love you.
C.A.*

AFRICAN POETRY BOOK SERIES

SERIES EDITOR

Kwame Dawes

EDITORIAL BOARD

Chris Abani, Northwestern University
Gabeba Baderoon, Pennsylvania State University
Kwame Dawes, University of Nebraska–Lincoln
Phillippa Yaa de Villiers, University of the Witwatersrand
Bernardine Evaristo, Brunel University
Aracelis Girmay, Stanford University
John Keene, Rutgers University
Matthew Shenoda, Brown University

ADVISORY BOARD

Laura Sillerman
Glenna Luschei
Elizabeth Alexander
Sulaiman Adebowale

TISA: NEW-GENERATION AFRICAN POETS

Introduction by Kwame Dawes and Chris Abani

CONTENTS OF BOX SET

At the Gates
Hazem Fahmy

Grief and Ecstasy
Rabha Ashry

Hairpins
Alain Jules Hirwa

here, there, and what is broken in between
Nneoma Veronica Nwogu

Learning to Say My Name
Nikitta Dede Adjirakor

A Litany on Loss
Tawiah Naana Akua Mensah

Maceration
Jay Kophy

Rose Ash
Samuel A. Adeyemi

The Sign of the Ram
O-Jeremiah Agbaakin

Speaking in Code
Phodiso Modirwa

What Still Yields
Jakky Bankong-Obi

NEW-GENERATION AFRICAN POETS (TISA)
Introduction
by Kwame Dawes and Chris Abani

PART ONE

Every year, Chris Abani and I find ourselves returning to a core question that forces us to consider the state of African poetry. The year is typically spent considering where things were when we started to think about an enterprise like the African Poetry Book Fund, and where we are now. In many ways, every new box set offers us a moment to think about what Africans are doing in poetry and where things are with the publishing of African poets. In this sense, the ritual of reviewing the manuscripts of emerging African poets is refreshing, for it affirms that Africans have never stopped finding ways to exist through the making of poems, the speaking of poems, and the business of contending with our lived world through language and the sharing of poetry. When this current box set appears, we will have published over 100 poets from Africa and of African descent in the space of eight years. Each year, the list of poets we approach for recommendations of emerging poets doing interesting work grows and spreads farther and farther around the continent and outside of it.

This is exciting. It does represent possibility. And rather than dwell on the sad state of affairs that would lead to a project like this having such an impact so quickly, I certainly would rather dwell on the beautiful ways in which African poetry is appearing in so many places where it was once quite rare. Here in the US, more and more African poets are being published by mainstream publishers and in many literary journals. They are winning awards, and they are developing their own communities and movements of poetry—organizing anthologies, creating websites, creating their own literary journals and much else—in ways that speak to the increased impact of the work we are doing.

Many of the poets who are engaged in this work, and whose work we see appearing around the country and in the UK, are poets we published first in our chapbook series, or poets who were finalists in the Evaristo African Poetry Prize, the Sillerman First Book Prize for African Poets, and in various anthologies that we have published. But the APBF has effectively sought to expand its work in as organic a manner as possible. We recently received a generous grant from the Poetry Foundation to study poetry book distribution in Africa, venturing into an area of publishing that is not often studied, and about which we do not ask the difficult questions.

We are publishing poets, but is their work getting around? African publishers are publishing African poets, but does their work have a chance to be distributed to festivals, booksellers, bookstores, and libraries in Africa? We have hunches, but we don't know, and so we will try to find out. We are also pushing hard to create a landscape in which the poets we have collected here will thrive—an ecosystem that ensures that their work is received, studied, preserved, shared, and valued during their lifetime and long after they have gone. We have to think in this way. It is this idea, this impetus for a living archive. It is a deliberate act of affirming the long tradition of poetry from Africa and in finding ways to consider that its evolving and transformative present moment must be accounted for and preserved. We are also deeply aware of the fact that much of what we are doing now finds us navigating these matters in English. We are aware that what constitutes African poetry in English is a mere fraction of possibility when we consider the presence of poetry in Africa in the past and now. So, we have already began our work on translation and on offering what we can to start us all thinking about poetry in African languages, even as we embrace the notion (normally attributed to Achebe) that English, and French, and Portuguese, and Spanish, etc. are African languages. In this sense, we have a catholic view of things, embracing the idea that the whole conception of Africa and Africanness is one that is constantly evolving, and one that is profoundly and radically expanding. In this sense, the work we do is radical in that it imposes on the rest of the world the creative force, spiritual complexity, and intellectual sophistication of various cultures and histories that have emerged in Africa and that continue to evolve, transform, and delight millions of people who are living day-to-day in those worlds.

This year's box set continues the work of expanding our opportunity to read writers from areas of Africa that have not been as well-represented in the previous box sets. Two of our poets, Hazem Fahmy and Rabha Ashry, are Egyptians, though the latter was born in Abu Dhabi. We are publishing our first Rwandan poet, Alain Jules Hirwa, and it is good to have Botswanan poet Phodiso Modirwa featured in this box set. Nigeria continues to produce poets of varied styles and themes, and four of them, Samuel Adeyemi, O-Jeremiah Agbaakin, Nneoma Veronica Nwogu, and Jakky Bankong-Obi, are featured in this box set. Three poets from Ghana are featured here, as well: Jay Kophy, Tawiah Mensah, and Nikitta Dede Adjirakor.

We remain deeply moved by the quality of work that we see in this process year after year. The eleven poets included here were drawn from about forty-eight solicited manuscripts that we received this year, based on recommendations from our community of poets, critics, and arts organizers. We have continued to pay attention to poets whose work has appeared in journals and other forums, and we have also relied on poets whose work has emerged in our various contests. We continue to look for ways to ensure that we are reaching more poetry communities around Africa, and our hope is to continue to provide a platform for these poets through our various projects.

—*Kwame Dawes*

PART TWO

My desire to assist in developing a living archive is a deep and abiding one. Living archives are seen as part of the praxis of social (in this case, artistic as well) memory and transmission. We can say for instance that a living archive refers to practices and conditions, even environments, that connect curation to transmission that is performative, participatory, and always creative. By its very nature, it is community bound and based and must be reflexive in real time.

Growing up as a young reader and writer in West Africa, I was privileged to have access to several book series. The famous Heinemann African Writers Series, edited by Chinua Achebe and later by Abdulrazak Gurnah, was an incredibly robust and important series that was published from 1962 up through the early 2000s. Almost every writer who makes up the first modern wave of African Writers, three who went on to win Nobel Prizes, including Abdulrazak, were first published in the Heinemann series. The writers hailed from Egypt to South Africa, from the Eastern coast to the West, and all the points within. The series focused mostly on fiction but the occasional poet made the cut, and we have republished several of those in our own series. The Heinemann series was over five hundred books long. No small thing.

Then there was the Pacesetter Series by Macmillan. It was a series of novellas, but with the scope of full novels, that focused on genre fiction for young adults. This series inspired my first book, *Masters of the Board*. They had about one hundred titles.

The third series was by Longman, and it was aimed squarely at college and high school course adoption. They curated a lot of post-Civil War books, and many of the historical and social works around this rupture in Nigeria's history were published there.

There were a few other local publishers taking stabs at this time, though they didn't run specific series and had varied editorial lists. Notably Fagbamigbe Publishing, whose star writer, Louis Omotayo Johnson, sold nearly a hundred thousand copies of his detective series books, which in '90s Nigeria was nothing short of a miracle. Then there was Spectrum, who didn't really rise to any real intervention because they were caught between a desire for trade publishing and the rarified air of textbook publishing. Finally, of note, was Delta, run by Nigerian writer Dillibe Onyeama. Delta published my first novel.

There are several things you may notice here. First is that Nigeria and Nigerians get mentioned a lot. This isn't because of any chauvinism on my part, but simply because with the biggest population on the continent, and one of the most vibrant and successful economies, Nigeria exerts an overly large impact on all areas of continental life. In fact, Nobel Prize Winner Nadine Gordimer of South Africa is quoted as saying that 70 percent of African literature is Nigerian literature. This is not to say there weren't interventions in other countries—Weaver Press from Zimbabwe is a notable one, and there were many from South Africa. I am speaking, however, of curated and enduring series. The second thing you may notice is that these series seldom include any poetry or poets, which is what makes what we do unique, important, and bearing the weight of many years of urgency.

You may wonder why you are getting this history lesson. There are multiple reasons. The first is that for a writer to combat the crushing weight of western literary hegemonies, an accessible tradition and an archive of that tradition is needed beyond what words can express. To find innovation, tradition, and the span of history within a literary culture that is DNA-deep is an incredible opportunity.

Then there are the three main parts of a living archive that keep it relevant and ever expanding (outside of the constant drive for funds and publishing partnerships) and these are:

1. The Historical Narrative: With time this builds itself, but with careful planning we have started to draw books and writers back into print from the periods covered by initial series and archives, with the hope of sustaining this, giving as big a historical narrative span backward and forward in time as we can. And we hope to hand this off soon to a new generation.
2. Current Reelections and Planning: We see through these introductions the conversations that develop across and between books and poets, and how these shape and drive the content of the work. It allows us to see what the current conversations are and how best to curate and organize.
3. Real Time Feedback: We can pivot, change, expand, and open more curatorial, editorial, and publishing spaces based on the feedback from all work that is submitted to us, including any work we publish. And based on the work we review, we can look at what education and training could be useful.

Where all the other series that I spoke of were by foreign companies and publishing endeavors, ours is fully African-driven and not owned for profit.

We plan for an ongoing home for contemporary African poetry, and with time we hope to find ourselves in a place where we can purchase and reintroduce the series from Heinemann, Longman, and Macmillan.

In just over eight years, we have published over 100 hundred chapbooks, and if we include the larger parts of the African Poetry Book Fund, that's about 150 writers. It seems a lot, but this is nothing given the size of the talent pool on the continent. It is at best a calling card. We hope to partner on the continent with more publishing collectives and endeavors so that the archive will grow, becoming so decentralized that it can never die. A living archive for the ages.

—Chris Abani

KWAME DAWES is the author of numerous books of poetry and other works of fiction, criticism, and essays. His most recent collection *unHistory*, was cowritten with John Kinsella. Dawes is a George W. Holmes University Professor of English and Glenna Luschei Editor of *Prairie Schooner*. He teaches in the Pacific MFA Program and is the series editor of the African Poetry Book Series, director of the African Poetry Book Fund, and artistic director of the Calabash International Literary Festival. He is a Chancellor for the Academy of American Poets and a Fellow of the Royal Society of Literature. Dawes is the winner of the prestigious Windham/Campbell Award for Poetry and was a finalist for the 2022 Neustadt International Prize for Literature. In 2022, Kwame Dawes was awarded the Order of Distinction Commander class by the Government of Jamaica.

CHRIS ABANI's prose includes *The Secret History of Las Vegas*, *Song for Night*, *The Virgin of Flames*, *Becoming Abigail*, *GraceLand*, and *Masters of the Board*. His poetry collections include *Smoking the Bible*, *Sanctificum*, *There Are No Names for Red*, *Feed Me the Sun*, *Hands Washing Water*, *Dog Woman*, *Daphne's Lot*, and *Kalakuta Republic*. He holds a BA and MA in English, an MA in gender and culture, and a PhD in literature and creative writing. Abani is the recipient of a PEN USA Freedom to Write Award, a Prince Claus Award, a Lannan Literary fellowship, a California Book Award, a Hurston/Wright Legacy Award, a PEN Beyond Margins Award, a PEN/Hemingway Award, and a Guggenheim fellowship; and he is a member of the American Academy of Arts and Sciences. Born in Nigeria, he is currently on the board of trustees, a professor of English, and director of African Studies at Northwestern University.

Victor Ekpuk is an internationally renowned Nigerian-American artist based in Washington, DC. His paintings, drawings, and sculptures reimagine the ancient Nigerian communication system, Nsibidi, to explore a diverse spectrum of meaning addressing historical narratives, the contemporary African diaspora, and humanity's connection to the sacred. Ekpuk's three-decade long career has earned his works inclusion in numerous prestigious collections, including the Smithsonian National Museum of African American History and Culture; Smithsonian National Museum of African Art; Boston Museum of Fine Art; The World Bank; Bank ABC (Arab Banking Corporation) in the Kingdom of Bahrain; Kiran Nadar Museum of Art in New Delhi; Elizabeth Miller Sculpture Center; Hood Museum of Art; Krannert Art Museum; Newark Museum of Art; and Art in Embassies. In recent years, Ekpuk has added large-scale murals, installations, and public art projects to his portfolio. He has been commissioned by The Phillips Collection, Washington, DC, North Carolina Museum of Art, Memphis Brooks Museum, Washington, DC, city government for Boone Elementary School, and Bank ABC (Arab Banking Corporation).